Note to Parents

Simply Science, the Independent level of the *Now I'm Reading!*™ series, offers five high-interest stories that allow children to gain reading fluency, confidence, and independence. Each story includes age-appropriate factual science content. The stories also provide ample opportunity for the growing reader to practice reading short- and long-vowel words as well as more challenging sounds, blends, and word skills.

Children also will learn new science vocabulary words related to each story subject. Before reading these stories, review the vocabulary words with your child so they become recognizable when reading. Also, discuss the science concept of each story with your child and what he or she knows about each topic.

For more information on how to use these stories with your child, refer to the pages at the end of this book.

NOW I'M READING!™

SIMPLY SCIENCE

INDEPENDENT ■ **VOLUME 1**

Hardcover Bind-up Edition
copyright © 2003, 2006 by innovativeKids®
All rights reserved
Published by innovativeKids®
A division of innovative USA®, Inc.
18 Ann Street
Norwalk, CT 06854
Printed in China

Conceived, developed, and designed
by the creative team at innovativeKids®
www.innovativekids.com

No part of this publication may be reproduced, stored in, or introduced into a retrieval system, or transmitted, in any form or by any means (electronic, mechanical, photocopying, recording, or otherwise), without the prior written permission of the publisher of this book.

For permission to use any
part of this publication, contact
innovativeKids®
Phone: 203-838-6400
Fax: 203-855-5582
E-mail: info@innovativekids.com

SIMPLY SCIENCE

Volume 1

Table of Contents

STORY 1 **BLAST OFF!**

STORY 2 **BONES**

STORY 3 **OUR PLANET**

STORY 4 **WATCH IT GROW**

STORY 5 **THE CHANGING CATERPILLAR**

STORY 1

BLAST OFF!

Written by Nora Gaydos
Illustrated by Lee Montgomery

3-2-1 Blast off! Zoom through outer space and see what you can explore.

The Sun is a big ball of burning gas. It is very hot and very bright. It warms Earth and gives us daylight.

Look at the Moon. The Moon is large and rocky. Its shape seems to change from night to night.

A planet is a large body of rock and gas. Mercury is the closest planet to the Sun. Next comes Venus, hot and cloudy.

Earth

Earth is where we live. It's the only planet with air, lots of water, and life.

Mars is red and closest to Earth. Jupiter is the largest planet. Saturn is the planet with bright rings around it.

Uranus and Neptune are big planets that are very cold. Pluto is the smallest planet and furthest from the Sun.

Our solar system is made up of the Sun, nine planets, and lots of moons.

The planets move around the Sun in paths called orbits.

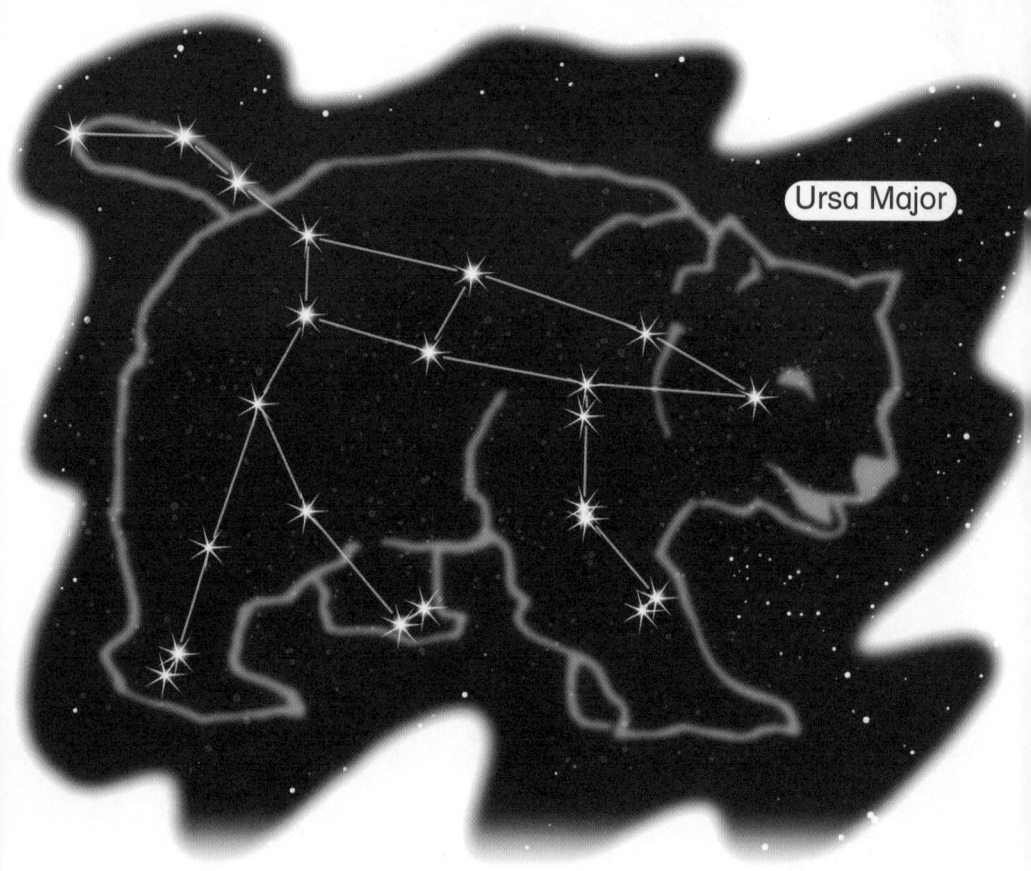

Past the planets are lots of bright stars. A group of stars that forms a picture is called a constellation.

Racing around in outer space is great. There is so much to see. But there's no place like home!

STORY 2

BONES

Written by Nora Gaydos
Illustrated by Marcelo Elizalde

What if you didn't have any bones in your body? You would be as floppy as a rag doll.

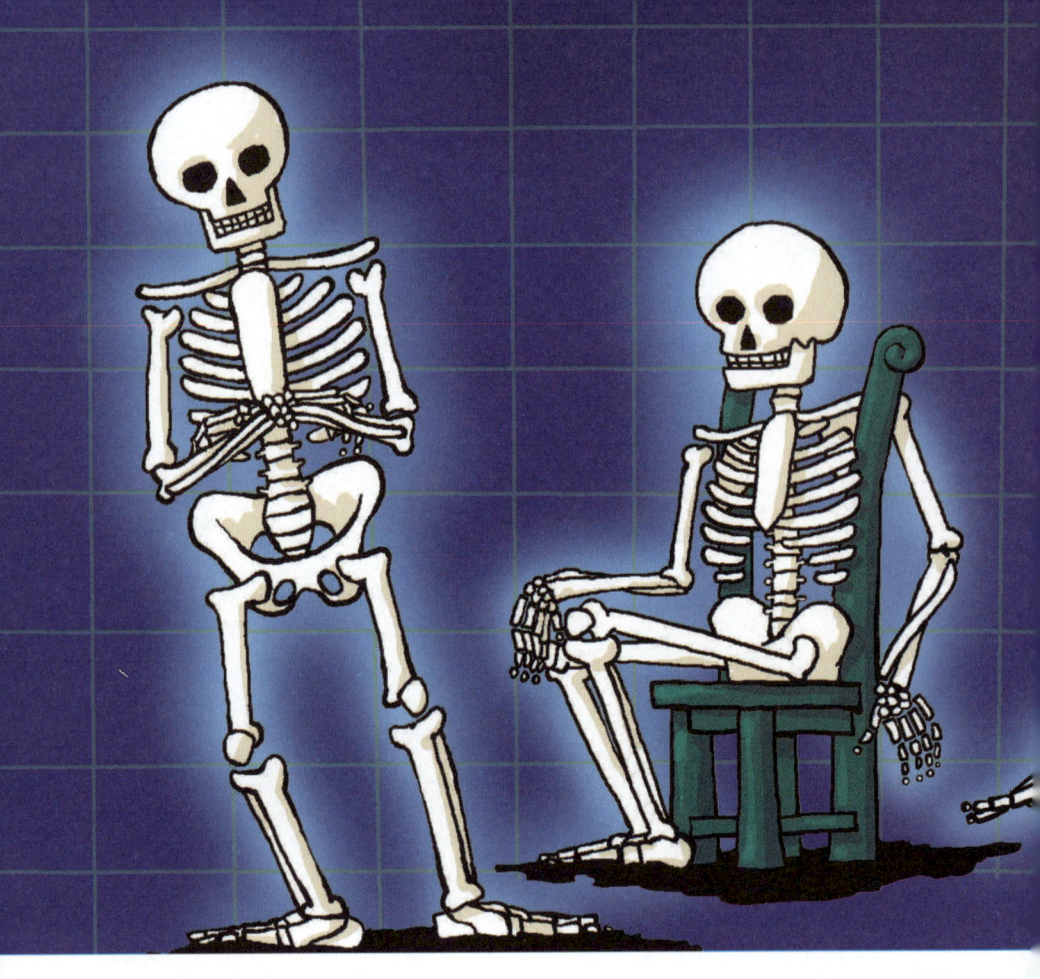

Your bones give your body shape. All of your bones make up your skeleton.

Your skeleton helps you stand, sit, run, walk, and bend.

Each bone connects to another bone at places called joints.

Bones and joints help different body parts move. Hand bones and joints make fingers move.

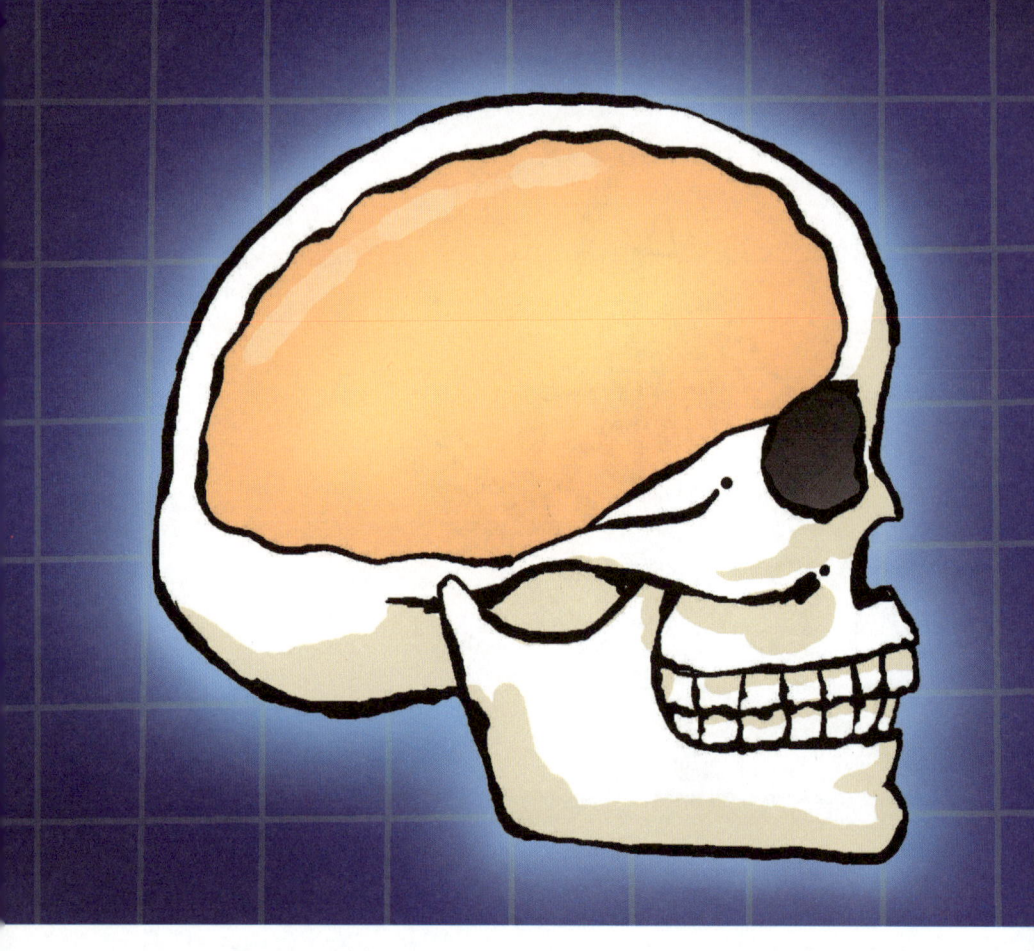

Bones are hard and protect the soft insides of your body. Your skull protects your brain, eyes, and ears.

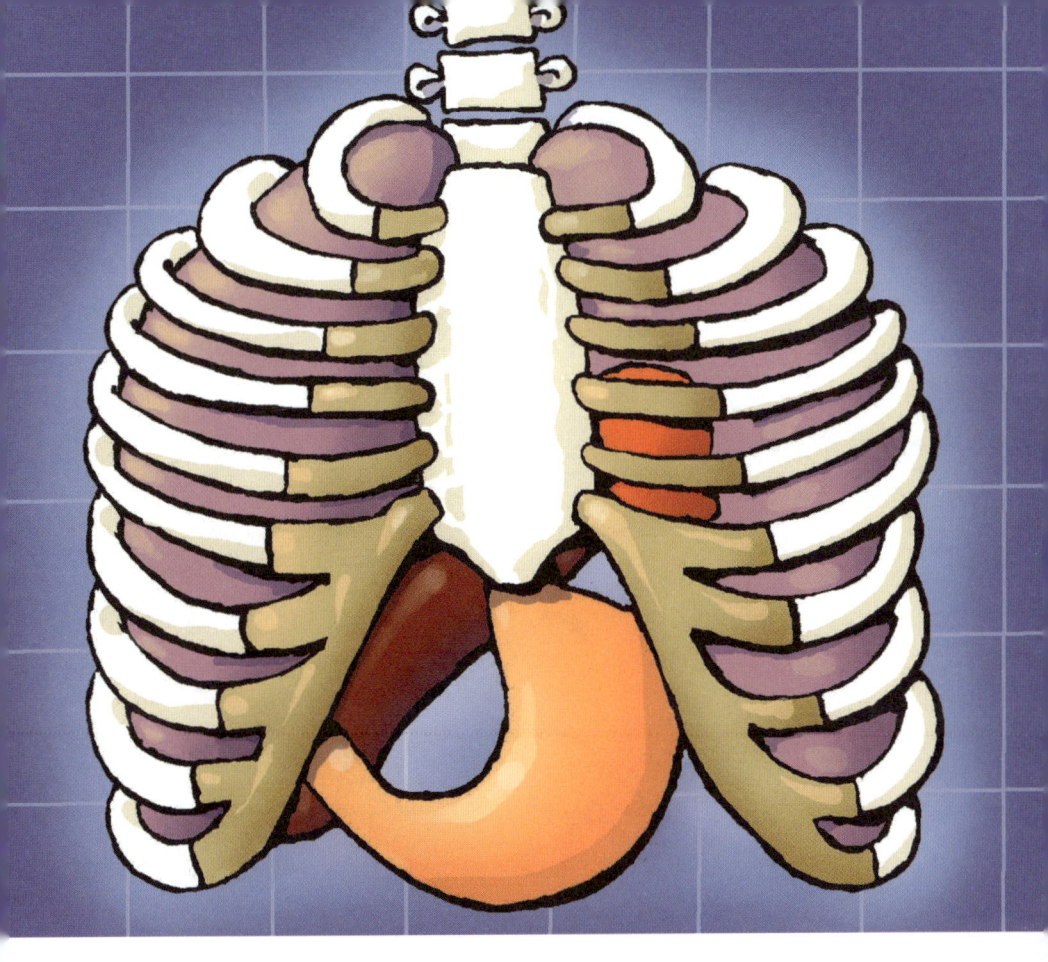

Your rib cage protects your lungs, heart, stomach, liver, and lots of other organs.

Bones can break. The doctor can see if you have a broken bone with an x-ray machine.

Bones can heal. The doctor can set the broken bone and hold it in place with a hard cast.

Drinking milk is good for your bones.
It makes them hard and strong.

Strong bones help you do all the things you like to do.

■ **STORY 3** ■

OUR PLANET

Written by Nora Gaydos
Illustrated by Doug Bowles

Imagine you are flying high over the earth. What would you see?

You would see large land areas called continents. You would see large water areas called oceans.

The oceans are salty and filled with many kinds of fish. The oceans cover most of the earth's surface.

You would see mountains that are higher than the land around them. Some are rocky or covered with trees.

You would see plains that are flat places on the earth. Many animals run across the green and grassy plains.

You would see forests full of tall trees. Many different plants and animals live in forests.

You would see rain forests that are wet and hot. Some animals live in the treetops. Some live on the ground.

You would see deserts that are large, dry places on the earth. Some are covered with sand and are very hot.

You would see glaciers that are huge sheets of ice. They cover cold and snowy lands.

You would see people, plants, and animals that live on the earth.

What a ride! What is the earth's land like where you live?

STORY 4

WATCH IT GROW

Written by Nora Gaydos
Illustrated by Geraldo Valério

Have you ever thought about growing your own plants and flowers? It's easy.

Plants are living things that grow almost anywhere—in water, in deserts, and in your backyard.

Plants come in all shapes and sizes.
Some have leaves. Some have flowers.
Some have fruits.

Flowering plants have four parts: roots, stems, leaves, and flowers.

Plants need air, sunlight, water, and food to grow.

Plants with flowers make seeds. A seed is a tiny case with a baby plant inside it.

To grow a plant, bury the seed under some soil. Water the soil where the seed was planted.

Soon, roots sprout from the seed and spread underground. The plant takes in food and water through the roots.

The new baby plant breaks through the seed. Then a little stem pushes up through the soil.

Leaves begin to sprout from the stem.
A bud forms and a flower blooms.

Plant some seeds in your backyard and watch them grow.

STORY 5

THE CHANGING CATERPILLAR

Written by Nora Gaydos
Illustrated by Ka Botzis

This garden is full of butterflies. Watch one and see what it does.

The butterfly lands on a leaf. It lays an egg on the leaf and flies away.

Soon, a caterpillar with many legs crawls out of the egg.

The caterpillar is hungry and starts to eat the green leaves around it. It eats more leaves and grows bigger.

As the caterpillar gets bigger, it sheds its skin so it can grow some more. At last, the caterpillar stops eating.

It attaches to a leaf or stem and starts to form a hard shell. This shell is called a chrysalis.

Once the chrysalis is complete, you cannot see the caterpillar for days, weeks, or months.

Inside the chrysalis, the caterpillar slowly changes into a butterfly.

In time, the butterfly tries to come out of the chrysalis.

Its wings are wet and droopy. Then they begin to dry out and uncurl.

The butterfly opens its wings and flies away. Where do you think it will go?

How to Use This Book

Prepare by reading the stories ahead of time. Familiarize yourself with the skills reinforced in each story. By doing this, you can better guide your child in recognizing the new words and sounds as they appear in the text.

Before reading, look at the pictures with your child. Encourage him or her to tell the story through the pictures. Next, read the books aloud to your child. Point to the words as you read to promote a connection between the spoken word and the printed word.

Have your child read to you. Encourage him or her to point to the words as he or she reads. By doing so, your child will begin to understand that each word has a separate sound and is represented in a distinct way on the page.

Encourage your child to read independently. This is the ultimate goal. Have him or her read alone or read aloud to other family members and friends.

▪ ▪ ▪ The Now I'm Reading!™ Series ▪ ▪ ▪

The *Now I'm Reading!*™ series integrates the best of phonics and literature-based reading. Phonics emphasizes letter-sound relationships, while a literature-based approach brings the enjoyment and excitement of a real story. The series has six reading levels:

Pre-Reader: Children "read" simple, patterned, and repetitive text and use picture clues to help them along.

Level 1: Children learn short vowel sounds, simple consonant sounds, and common sight words.

Level 2: Children learn long and short vowel sounds, more consonants and consonant blends, plus more sight word reinforcement.

Level 3: Children learn new vowel sounds, with more consonant blends, double consonants, and longer words and sentences.

Level 4: Children learn advanced word skills, including silent letters, multi-syllable words, compound words, and contractions.

Independent: Children are introduced to high-interest topics as they tackle challenging vocabulary words and information by using previous phonics skills.

Reading Comprehension

Blast Off!
1. How many planets are in our solar system?
2. What is the name of a group of stars that forms a picture?

Bones
3. What body parts does your skull protect?
4. How does your skeleton help you?

Our Planet
5. How are deserts different from rain forests?
6. What covers most of the Earth's surface?

Watch It Grow
7. What are the four parts of a flowering plant?
8. What do plants need in order to grow?

The Changing Caterpillar
9. What hatches from a butterfly's egg?
10. What is the name of the hard shell that forms around the caterpillar?

Vocabulary

Chrysalis - the hard shell that caterpillars form and stay in while they turn into a butterfly

Constellation - a group of stars that forms a picture

Continents - large land areas

Deserts - large, dry areas that are usually sandy and hot

Joints - the place where bones connect to other bones

Plains - flat, grassy areas

Planet - a large body of rock and gas

Skeleton - the support system of bones that gives your body shape and protects your soft insides

Solar system - the sun and the nine planets that orbit around it

About the Author

Nora Gaydos is an elementary school teacher with more than ten years of classroom experience teaching kindergarten, first grade, and third grade. She has a broad understanding of how beginning readers develop from the earliest stage of pre-reading to becoming independent, self-motivated readers. Nora has a degree in elementary education from Miami University in Ohio and lives in Connecticut with her husband and two sons. Nora is also the author of *Now I Know My ABCs* and *Now I Know My 1, 2, 3's,* as well as other early-learning concept books published by innovativeKids®.